A Personal Skills Course

CONFLICT
Shay McConnon

MACMILLAN EDUCATION

© Shay McConnon 1990

All rights reserved. No reproduction, copy or transmission of this
publication may be made without written permission.

No paragraph of this publication may be reproduced, copied or
transmitted save with written permission or in accordance with the
provisions of the Copyright, Designs and Patents Act 1988, or
under the terms of any licence permitting limited copying
issued by the Copyright Licensing Agency, 33–4 Alfred Place,
London WC1E 7DP.

The photocopying of some pages is permitted. These pages are
marked thus Ⓟ. However, only reasonable quantities of
photocopies can be made and these should be for internal school
use only. Under no circumstances can large numbers of copies be
made either by schools or LEAs.

Any person who does any unauthorised act in relation to this
publication may be liable to criminal prosecution and
civil claims for damages.

First edition 1990
Reprinted 1990

Published by
MACMILLAN EDUCATION LTD
Houndmills, Basingstoke, Hampshire RG21 2XS
and London
Companies and representatives
throughout the world

Illustrated by Nick Oates and Bob Moulder

Printed in Great Britain by
Cathedral Press Ltd, Salisbury, Wiltshire

British Library Cataloguing in Publication Data
McConnon, Shay
  Conflict. — (Your choice)
  1. Social conflict
  I. Title   II. Series
  303.6

ISBN 0–333–51119–0

CONTENTS

Conflict would appear to be an inevitable part of life. It exists at global, local and personal levels. Young people who experience conflict at home, in school or with friends, can often lack the skills to handle these conflicts in satisfactory ways. This course gives students opportunities to learn and practise the skills of conflict resolution.

Conflicts can be handled in four basic ways: aggression, withdrawal, mediation and negotiation. Negotiation, which respects both parties' needs, and views the conflict as a shared problem, is generally the most helpful way of resolving conflict.

For the purpose of this course, conflict can be taken to mean a clash of ideas, wishes, needs or interests. Although often seen in destructive terms resulting in violence, stress and unhappiness, conflict can also be creative and lead to greater self-respect and improved personal relationships.

This course offers a programme of structured experiences which aim to prepare students to deal with conflicts in positive ways. It helps them to understand why conflicts occur, how they can be escalated or defused and teaches successful ways of handling them.

Strategy 1

The opening strategy encourages students to reflect on their experience of conflict and share thoughts and feelings on a variety of conflict issues.

Strategies 2–3

The extent and range of conflict in the world at international, local and personal levels are explored. Students identify conflict situations which are typical in the lives of young people.

Strategies 4–6

Students examine how people normally respond to conflicts, identify behaviours which escalate and those which defuse conflicts, and decide on the most successful way of resolving conflicts.

Strategies 7–8

The skills of negotiation are taught and practised, and feedback given on their use.

Strategies 9–10

Students decide on ways of reducing existing conflict in their lives and look at practical ways of preventing conflicts from arising.

Strategy 11

Students assess their conflict management skills, establish behaviour goals and are given the opportunity to commit themselves to these goals using a structured plan for behaviour change.

Strategy 12

The programme concludes with an evaluation of the student's personal response to the exercises in this book.

Appendix

The appendix suggests two strategies for handling persistent conflicts. These can be used by the teacher to resolve an ongoing conflict between students. Although positive and useful strategies, they should be used with caution and only when all parties consent.

Most of the strategies involve small group work. The group can be the teacher's most effective resource in helping students to become aware of their conflict management styles. The group also provides opportunities to experiment with new behaviours and receive feedback on them. Such work, however, requires sensitive handling by the teacher, who needs to create a positive, non-critical atmosphere in which individuals feel valued and listened to.

The time suggested for each strategy is an approximate guideline. The ability and maturity of the students will determine how long each strategy takes. Each strategy is divided into several phases which provide a natural break for limited time sessions. Most strategies include ideas for variations on the main procedure or a development of the exercise. Although the exercises are suitable across a wide age range, the teacher might wish to modify the content to make them more relevant to a specific group.

PROFILING

Recent initiatives in education encourage a move towards profiling, continuous assessment and reviewing. Assessment is to be seen as an integral part of all learning experiences. The student is at the centre of this process and its success requires that students understand the assessment procedure and are involved in the assessment process. Giving students a copy of their profile statements at the beginning of the course allows them to become aware of the assessment objectives. By explaining these objectives and the assessment procedure, students will know what to assess themselves on and how.

The review is a key element in effective profiling. Ideally this should take place at regular intervals during the course, rather than leaving the review to the end.

The students' completed worksheets could be used to form part of their formative profile and provide useful moments for reviewing with the student.

The teacher may wish to involve parents in this process and design the profile to allow them to make written comments.

The teacher could also design a scheme which asks students to assess themselves at the end of each session, e.g.

				Sessions					
	1	2	3	4	5	6	7	8
I work without supervision	8	6	7					
I work to the best of my ability	7	5						
I am keen to learn	7	7						

Students score themselves out of ten for each of these skill areas. Over a period of time, students will get a picture of themselves and be able to note areas of success along with skills needing attention. This can then be reviewed with the teacher.

However the profile is designed or executed, students hopefully will feel that their formative profiles are a tool they can use to become more aware of self, to monitor progress and then decide on new starting points.

The profile statement which follows is in two parts. (A) is an assessment sheet for skills taught during the course. (B) is an assessment sheet for students' attitudes and their ability to co-operate with each other. Each sheet allows both teacher and student to make independent comments on progress. These can be used as a basis for a review resulting in a joint comment.

PROFILE STATEMENT (A): CONFLICT

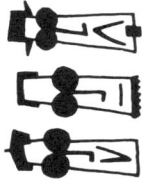

Name _____

Date _____

			COMMENTS
1	I can talk to the group about my thoughts and feelings on conflict.		
2	I know how conflicts can be resolved or made worse.		
3	I am aware of the skills of negotiation.		
4	I can use these skills successfully.		
5	I am aware of the conflict in my own life.		
6	I know which of these conflicts I can prevent and which I need to manage better.		
7	I can draw up a goal plan to reduce conflict in my life.		

STUDENT

Report on the progress you have made:

TEACHER

Report on this student's progress:

JOINT COMMENTS

After discussion, we have agreed that progress has been made in:

But attention needs to be paid to:

The following action has been agreed on:

Signed _____ TEACHER

Signed _____ STUDENT

Ⓟ © Shay McConnon 1990

4

PROFILE STATEMENT (B): CONFLICT

Name _____ Date _____

ATTITUDE AND WORKING WITH OTHERS

> Indicate your attitude marking the continuum line with an X.
> The teacher will score your attitude on this line with an O.

	Always		Sometimes			Never
I work without supervision.						
I work to the best of my ability.						
I am keen to learn.						
I organise myself.						
I make good use of the time available.						
I co-operate with other students.						
I try to involve the quieter members.						
I make suggestions and offer ideas.						
I listen attentively to others.						
I help the group make decisions.						
I talk with confidence in the group.						
I try to understand other students' points of view.						

What I do well is:

What I could do better is:

Ⓟ © Shay McConnon 1990

MODULE OVERVIEW

CHAPTER	DESCRIPTION	TYPE OF ACTIVITY	TIME	SIZE OF GROUP	WORK-SHEETS	ADDITIONAL MATERIALS	WORK EXTEN-SION
1 This Is Me	Thoughts and feelings on a variety of conflict issues are shared in small groups.	incomplete sentences	30	4–6	1	—	✓
2 Our Troubled World	The extent and range of conflict in the world is examined.	collage/discussion	40–45	3–4	—	newspapers, magazines, scissors, glue, paper	✓
3 Typical Conflicts	Conflicts that arise in the lives of young people are identified.	decision making/brainstorm	30–40	4–5	—	paper, markers, labelled cards	✓
4 Typical Responses	Common ways of handling conflict are examined.	question and answer/role-play	40–45	pairs/3–4	2	—	✓
5 Hot And Cold	Responses likely to escalate and those likely to defuse conflicts are identified.	analysis/brainstorm/rank order	40–45	2–3/5–6	2	paper, markers	✓
6 Which Way Is Best?	The four basic ways of handling conflict are examined and evaluated.	flowchart/analysis	30–40	individuals/3–4	2	—	✓
7 Negotiate!	The skills of successful negotiation are taught and practised.	role-play/skill practice/discussion	30–40	pairs	2	—	✓
8 Let's Agree	Students are given further opportunity to practise the skills of negotiation and receive feedback on their use of these skills.	consensus	45	12	2	tokens	✓
9 Conflict In My Life	Students identify a conflict which causes them concern and decide on ways of handling it.	questionnaire/role-play/analysis	50–60	individuals/pairs/4–5	2	—	✓
10 Preventing Conflict	Attention is drawn to 'avoidable conflicts' and to ways of preventing them.	analysis/discussion	30–40	3–4	3	—	✓
11 What Now?	Students identify target behaviours and commit themselves to these.	assessment/goal setting	40–50	4–5/varies	3	—	✓
12 How Have We Got On?	An assessment of students' responses to these exercises.	evaluation	30–40	varies	1	—	✓

Aim:
To help students share thoughts and feelings on a variety of conflict issues.

Procedure:

- **Phase I**
  - Give each student the worksheet **THIS IS ME**.
  - Explain the task and give examples of completed sentences.
  - Allow time for students to complete the sentences.
  - Form groups of 4–6.
  - Students take it in turn to read out the first completed sentence. The others are to listen without making comments.
  - Students are free to pass.
  - The second sentence is shared with the group and the procedure continues as above.

- **Phase II**
  - Reconvene the class and invite students to comment on what they have learned from each other, e.g.
    - How do students generally feel when they are called a name?
    - When they see two people fighting?
    - When someone jumps a bus queue? . . . and so on.

Extensions:

1 Turn this into a game. Transfer the incomplete sentences on to cards. Divide the class into groups of 4–6. Shuffle the cards. In turn, each student takes a card and completes the sentence. Students are free to pass or delay responding, allowing them time to give a satisfactory response.

2 The class forms two circles, an inner and an outer circle, with students facing each other in pairs. Read aloud one of the incomplete sentences. Each student completes it with his partner. Continue for three sentences and then one circle moves to the left. Read out another three sentence stems and continue with the above procedure.

Group Size: 4–6

Time: Approximately 30 minutes

Materials: Each student requires:
- worksheet **THIS IS ME**

Notes:

The incomplete sentences focus attention on ways of handling conflict. Encourage students to answer honestly how they would react in the situations described on the worksheet. These answers can give an indication of how individual students respond to conflict. By repeating this exercise at the end of the course, students can make a comparison between the two sets of answers and note any changes.

This strategy can be used as a written homework assignment or as a stimulus for discussion work. It can be used at any stage during the course.

One way of using the strategy over several sessions is to group the incomplete sentences in blocks of five and ask the class to complete them at the beginning or end of a session.

THIS IS ME

Name _____   Date _____

1 When someone calls me a name I _____

2 When I don't get my own way I _____

3 When I see someone with a black eye I _____

4 When I see someone bully another I _____

5 When I row with my mum/dad I _____

6 When I see two people fighting I _____

7 When I am made to wash the dishes I _____

8 When I see a player question a referee's decision I _____
   _____

9 When someone is angry with me I _____

10 When I see something unfair happening I _____

11 When I am told off I _____

12 When I see two people shouting at each other I _____
   _____

13 When I see someone taking more than their fair share I _____
   _____

14 When I read of war in the newspapers I _____

15 When someone teases me I _____

16 When two people argue over where to sit I _____

17 When I arrive home later than the agreed time I _____
   _____

18 When I see someone jump a bus queue I _____

19 When I row with my teacher I _____

20 When someone doesn't want to do what I want I _____
   _____

8

Ⓟ © Shay McConnon 1990

2 OUR TROUBLED WORLD ■■■■

Aim: To help students become more aware of the extent and range of conflict in our world.

Procedure:

- **Phase I**
  - Form groups of 3–4.
  - Give each group a selection of magazines and newspapers, scissors, glue and a large sheet of paper which has been headed with one of the following titles:
    CONFLICT BETWEEN COUNTRIES
    CONFLICT BETWEEN GROUPS
    CONFLICT BETWEEN INDIVIDUALS.
  - Explain these different types of conflict, using examples from the newspapers/magazines.
  - Using photographs, headlines, articles etc., each group makes a collage to describe the type of conflict which is on their sheet of paper.

- **Phase II**
  - Reconvene the class.
  - Invite a representative from each group to show their collage to the class, explain/comment on it and be prepared to answer questions from the class.

- **Phase III**
  - Discuss with the class:
    - Should we be surprised to see so much conflict in the world?
    - How does the class react/feel on seeing this degree of conflict?
    - What can be done about it?
    - Is conflict sometimes necessary? Any examples?
    - How do students feel when they are in conflict?

Extensions:

1 Students carry out a survey of conflict on TV. They are to note frequency of incidents, how the conflicts are resolved and the role of violence.
2 Discuss a popular TV programme or comic magazine which is noted for its violence. Does violence appeal? What audience is being catered for? Is the portrayal of violence a good thing?
3 Students select an item of conflict (local, national or global) which is in the news. They follow the development of the conflict as reported on TV or in the newspapers, write a report on it and share this with the class.

Group Size: 3–4

Time: 40–45 minutes

Materials: Each student requires:
- large sheet of paper
- selection of newspapers and magazines
- scissors and glue

Notes:

By drawing attention to conflict at global, local and personal levels, it is hoped that students will become aware of the extent and range of conflict in our world and also develop a clearer picture of what conflict means.

For the purposes of this course, conflict can be taken to mean a clash of ideas, wishes, needs or interests between people. It is not necessarily a bad thing and often can have positive outcomes.

Examples of the various types of conflict might be:
- between countries, e.g. countries at war
- between groups, e.g. trade unions taking strike action against management
- between individuals, e.g. husband and wife getting divorced.

Students could be asked to make a collage as a homework assignment and share their work in small groups or with the class in a future session.

Aim: To identify conflicts that arise among young people.

Procedure:

- ● **Phase I**
  - ○ Make four cards labelled A LOT, SOMETIMES, SELDOM, NEVER in large, clear lettering.
  - ○ Prepare the room with a labelled card in each of the four corners, a central space for students to gather, and furniture arranged to allow students to move freely to each corner.
  - ○ Explain the strategy: after a conflict issue is read out, students decide whether they experience conflicts over this issue A LOT, SOMETIMES, SELDOM or NEVER, then go to the appropriate corner of the room when the signal is given.
  - ○ Class gathers in the centre of the room.
  - ○ Read out a conflict issue from this list (you can of course add your own issues):
    HOMEWORK, TIME KEEPING, MY FRIENDS, TIDINESS, BOY/GIRLFRIENDS, HAIRSTYLE, SCHOOL, BEHAVIOUR, PARENTS, BROTHER/SISTER, CLOTHES, BEDROOM, TELEVISION, TEACHERS, GRANDPARENTS.
  - ○ At a signal (e.g. a clap of hands or a whistle) students move to their chosen corner of the room.
  - ○ Ask students to volunteer examples/incidents.
  - ○ The class now returns to the centre of the room.
  - ○ Read out another conflict issue and continue as above.

- ● **Phase II**
  - ○ Form groups of 4–5.
  - ○ Give a large sheet of paper and a marker to each group.
  - ○ Each group chooses a secretary and a spokesperson.
  - ○ Each group brainstorms for typical conflict incidents from their lives.
  - ○ The secretary writes these on the paper provided.
  - ○ Allow 6–8 minutes for this.
  - ○ Each group then decides on the three most common conflict incidents.
  - ○ The secretary puts a star by these.

- ● **Phase III**
  - ○ Reconvene the class.
  - ○ Invite each spokesperson to comment to the class on the results of the brainstorm.
  - ○ Note on the blackboard/flipchart what each group considers to be the most common conflict incidents.
  - ○ Conclude by drawing attention to similarities between the lists.

Group Size: 4–5

Time: 30–40 minutes

Materials: Each group requires:
- ○ large sheet of paper and marker

The teacher requires:
- ○ list of conflict issues
- ○ four cards labelled A LOT, SOMETIMES, SELDOM, NEVER

Notes:

Having looked at the extent and range of conflict in the world, students are now asked to identify those conflict incidents that are commonly experienced by young people. These can then be used throughout this course for analysis, role-play and the practice of negotiation skills.

Phase I is an energetic exercise designed to stimulate students into thinking about conflict in their lives. It is followed by a brainstorm exercise (Phase II) where students are asked to give incidents of conflict they experience. Encourage students to be specific, e.g. 'My mum and I are constantly rowing over the clothes I wear' rather than 'I row with my mum'.

The brainstorm sheets could be left on display for the duration of the course and used as a resource, e.g. students who need to decide on an incident to role play can refer to the sheets.

The incidents of conflict identified in this session could replace the examples of conflict used in this book. In this way, teachers can feel confident that they are dealing with conflict situations relevant to the lives of their students.

Extensions:

1 Phase I can be extended by inviting each corner in turn to reveal the amount of stress caused by such conflict, e.g 'Hands up those for whom this conflict causes – a lot of upset, some upset, little upset. . .'.

2 Prepare large sheets of paper with various conflict headings, e.g. Time Keeping, My Bedroom. Spread the sheets around the room. Students are to wander around the room writing conflict incidents they have experienced under the appropriate headings.

Aim: To investigate how people normally respond to conflict.

Procedure:

● Phase I
○ Form pairs and decide who is to be A and B.
○ Give each student a **CONFLICT PICTURE**, which they are not to show to their partner. (A and B are not to receive the same picture.)
○ B describes her conflict picture to A.
○ A should try to find out:
  – Who is involved?
  – What is happening?
  – Where is it happening?
  – Why is it happening?
  – What does each person in the conflict want?
  – What is likely to happen next?
○ Allow time for this and then pairs swap roles.

● Phase II
○ Form groups of 3–4. (If 3–4 copies of the same picture were given out in Phase I then those with the same conflict picture could form a group.)
○ Each group is to role play the conflict depicted on the picture, introducing extra characters, if necessary, e.g. police officer, friend, shop assistant for the shoplifting situation.
○ Allow time for students to decide:
  – who is to play the various roles
  – what the conflict is about
  – how the conflict will develop.
○ Each group now takes it in turn to briefly role play their conflict scene.

● Phase III
○ Reconvene the class and discuss:
  – How typical are these incidents of conflict?
  – During the role-play, did the conflicts develop in realistic ways?
  – How did the various characters handle the conflict? How did they behave? What did they do?
  – Which was the most usual response to conflict?
  – Were any of the conflicts defused/resolved successfully? If so – which type of response resolved the conflict successfully? If not – what could the characters have done to have resolved the conflict?

Group Size: Pairs; 3–4

Time: 40–45 minutes

Materials: Each student requires:
○ 1 **CONFLICT PICTURE**

Notes:

The course progresses from identifying the conflicts that young people experience, to an exploration of how people normally respond to such conflicts.

It is not the intention at this stage to carry out an in-depth evaluation of conflict management styles. The strategy simply provides an opportunity for students to become aware of how people generally respond in conflict situations.

The question and answer activity in Phase I should help students look closely at the conflict pictures and think about the causes and likely outcomes of the conflicts.

It is important to allow groups time to prepare for the role-play. It gives students the opportunity to be clear about the conflict and decide on how it will develop.

Extensions:

1 Make a worksheet for each of the conflict pictures and add the following questions:
  – Who is involved?
  – What is happening?
  – Where is it happening?
  – What caused this conflict?
  – What does each person want?
  – What is likely to happen next?
  – What would you advise the characters to do to resolve the conflict?
  – How could the conflict have been prevented from arising in the first place?
  These worksheets could be completed either in the classroom or as homework, and the answers shared in small groups.

2 Ask students to role play different ways of handling the same conflict (e.g. getting loud, being aggressive, crying, running away, remaining calm, being assertive, hitting the person, and so on). The class can then evaluate these different styles of conflict management.

CONFLICT PICTURES

© D. C. Thomson & Co Ltd, 1987

© D. C. Thomson & Co Ltd, 1987

Ⓟ © Shay McConnon 1990

CONFLICT PICTURES

© Fleetway Publications, 1989

© D. C. Thomson & Co Ltd, 1987

© Fleetway Publications, 1989

© D. C. Thomson & Co Ltd, 1987

Ⓟ © Shay McConnon 1990

Aim:
To give students the opportunity to evaluate behaviours likely to escalate and those likely to defuse conflict.

Procedure:

- **Phase I**
  - Form groups of 2–3.
  - Each group chooses a secretary and a spokesperson.
  - Give each group the worksheet **CONFLICT IN THE PLAYGROUND**.
  - Each group completes the worksheet, the secretary writing answers in the spaces provided.
  - Reconvene the class and invite each spokesperson to report back on the group's answers.

- **Phase II**
  - Form groups of 5–6.
  - Each group chooses a secretary and a spokesperson.
  - Give each group a large sheet of paper and a marker.
  - Each group brainstorms for ideas on what Gary could do next, both likely and unlikely actions, e.g. run away, cry, hit Brendan etc.
  - The secretary writes these on the sheet.
  - Allow 5–6 minutes for this.
  - Reconvene the class and ask each spokesperson to report back.
  - Write the ideas on the blackboard/flipchart.

- **Phase III**
  - Re-form to the groups of 5–6.
  - Give each group the worksheet **HOT AND COLD**.
  - Each group decides which responses listed on the blackboard/flipchart are likely to escalate the conflict and which responses are likely to defuse the conflict, and lists these on the worksheet.
  - Each group stars the three responses most likely to escalate the conflict and the three responses most likely to defuse the conflict.
  - Reconvene the class and invite each group to report back.
  - Discuss with the class:
    - how conflict can escalate, and why
    - how conflict can be defused, and why.

Extensions:
1 Students rank order the responses on the chart opposite from 1 to 7. The action most likely to defuse a conflict scores 1. The action most likely to escalate a conflict scores 7. This is first carried out individually, then in pairs, fours and lastly eights.

Group Size: 2–3; 5–6

Time: 40–45 minutes

Materials: Each group of 2–3 requires:
- worksheet **CONFLICT IN THE PLAYGROUND**

  Each group of 5–6 requires:
- worksheet **HOT AND COLD**
- large sheet of paper and marker

	Personal	Pairs	Fours	Eights
Run away				
Hit the person				
Talk about the problem				
Call names				
Get someone else to help				
Cry				
Try to understand the person				

2 Play a video with clips of TV programmes showing conflict. Freeze frame at the moment of confrontation and ask students to decide what could happen next. In this way students can make a list of escalating and defusing responses.

3 Replace the worksheet **CONFLICT IN THE PLAYGROUND** with a story about conflict or a picture-strip showing a different conflict incident, e.g. two people arguing over a choice of TV programmes; two boys squaring up to each other after colliding in the playground; two pupils arguing over where to sit; a pupil refusing to let another copy his homework; a pupil arriving late for class; arriving home later than the agreed time; returning damaged goods to a reluctant shopkeeper; a boy wanting to go 'too far' in a relationship; jumping a bus queue; a person bullying; putting pressure on someone to smoke when he doesn't want to; making fun of a person because he goes to church.

Notes:

The previous strategy examined common ways of responding to conflict. In this strategy, students are given the opportunity to evaluate these responses — to decide which are likely to escalate and which are likely to defuse conflict.

Conflict is likely to escalate if there is an increase in anger, frustration or perceived threat. Conflict is likely to be defused if the *issue* is focused on rather than the personalities involved, and also if there is a decrease in anger, frustration and perceived threat.

The strategy is in three phases. It opens with an analysis of a conflict situation, possible responses are then decided on and these are then evaluated. The aim of the brainstorm in Phase II is to get a variety of escalating and defusing responses. To achieve this the teacher could also ask groups to brainstorm on what Brendan could do next or on what the teacher could do next.

CONFLICT IN THE PLAYGROUND could be role-played or replaced by a different situation. Possible alternatives are listed in the Extension.

CONFLICT IN THE PLAYGROUND

What does Brendan want? _____

What does Gary want? _____

What does Tommy want? _____

What does the teacher want? _____

Who is involved in the conflict? _____

What is the conflict about? _____

What has caused this conflict? _____

© D. C. Thomson & Co Ltd, 1987

Ⓟ © Shay McConnon 1990

HOT AND COLD

Decide which responses are likely to escalate the conflict and which ones are likely to defuse the conflict.

After you have made your two lists:
Star the *three* responses most likely to escalate the conflict.
Star the *three* responses most likely to defuse the conflict.

Write him a letter

Try and understand him

Call him names

Joke about it

Hit him

ESCALATING RESPONSES

1 _____
2 _____
3 _____
4 _____
5 _____
6 _____
7 _____
8 _____

DEFUSING RESPONSES

1 _____
2 _____
3 _____
4 _____
5 _____
6 _____
7 _____
8 _____

Cry

Swear

Run away

Talk about the problem

Get someone else to help

Get a gang involved

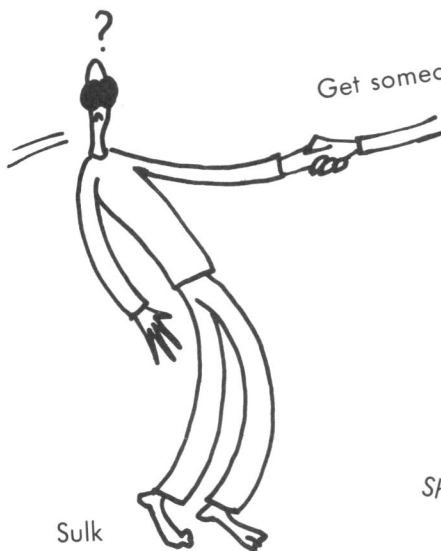

Sulk

Shout at him

Apologise

Be assertive

Ⓟ © Shay McConnon 1990

Aim: To help students examine and evaluate the four basic ways of handling conflict.

Procedure:

- **Phase I**
  - Copies of the completed worksheet **PETER AND SARAH** can be given to students or projected using an OHP.
  - Using this worksheet, explain the effects of aggression, mediation, withdrawal and negotiation on the development of a conflict situation.

- **Phase II**
  - Give each student the worksheet **WHICH WAY IS BEST?**
  - Suggest various conflict situations that the students could use (there are some possibilities in Strategies 3 and 5).
  - Each student decides on a conflict situation and completes the flowchart on the worksheet.
  - Form groups of 3–4.
  - Students take it in turn to share their completed worksheets.

- **Phase III**
  - Reconvene the class and discuss:
    - What are the consequences of aggression?
    - What are the consequences of mediation?
    - What are the consequences of withdrawal?
    - What are the consequences of negotiation?
    - Which approach is the most helpful? Why?
    - Which approach is the least helpful? Why?
    - Which way is best for conflict resolution?

Extensions:

1 Students are to observe conflict in the playground, classroom, at home etc. and look at the outcomes of the different ways of handling conflict. This can be given as a homework assignment, with students filling in boxes like the example opposite. Students can later discuss their findings in small groups and answer the question: 'Which way is best for conflict resolution?'

Group Size: Individuals; 3–4

Time: 30–40 minutes

Materials: Each student requires:
- worksheet **WHICH WAY IS BEST?**

The teacher requires:
- worksheet **PETER AND SARAH**

Notes:

Conflict can be handled in four basic ways: (a) aggression, (b) mediation, (c) withdrawal and (d) negotiation. Negotiation, which respects both parties' needs, and views the conflict as a shared problem, is generally the most helpful way of resolving conflict.

This strategy helps students to evaluate these four basic ways of handling conflict. Students should be encouraged to look at the consequences of these approaches and decide for themselves on their usefulness.

Phase II will have more meaning if students take an existing conflict which is causing anxiety and apply the four methods to this.

Conflict: Observer's sheet

Who was involved? _____

What was the conflict about? _____
_____

How was it handled? _____
_____

Was it resolved successfully? _____

---

2 Students keep a diary of the conflicts they experience (for one day/week) and note who it was with, the cause, how it was handled and what the outcomes were.

3 Give students a 'Dear Problem Page' letter that is asking for help on resolving a conflict. Students draft a reply offering suggestions for ways of handling this conflict successfully.

PETER AND SARAH

PETER AND SARAH ARE ARGUING OVER A CHOICE OF TV PROGRAMMES.

'Tomorrow's World is my favourite programme.'
'I don't care, I want to see *Coronation Street.'*

NEGOTIATION

Peter switches TV channels. Sarah turns the TV off.

Peter: What did you do that for?
Sarah: Because it's not fair.

Sarah: You want to watch *Coronation Street* and I want to see *Tomorrow's World.* The two programmes are on at the same time and we have only one TV.
Peter: OK, so that's why we argue every week.

Sarah: Why don't we take it in turn to have our choice of programmes?
Peter: Suppose so – provided I get to watch *Coronation Street* now.

WITHDRAWAL

Peter switches channels. Sarah goes up to her room and sulks.

MEDIATION

Peter switches channels. Sarah goes to get her mum.

Mum: What's wrong now?
Sarah: Peter keeps switching TV channels.

Mum: Peter, you were asked to clean the car. Now go and let Sarah watch the television.

AGGRESSION

Peter pushes Sarah away and switches channels.

Sarah: You've always got to get your own way.
Peter: Go away and have a cry.

Sarah: You're a bully and a pig.
Peter: Shut up before I hit you.

Sarah, in anger, throws a book at him.
Peter, furious, rushes after her.

Ⓟ © Shay McConnon 1990

WHICH WAY IS BEST ?

Name _____

Date _____

NEGOTIATION

WITHDRAWAL

MEDIATION

AGGRESSION

Ⓟ © Shay McConnon 1990

Aim: To help students become aware of the skills involved in successful negotiation and provide practice in these.

Procedure:

● Phase I
○ Recap on the importance of negotiation as a successful way of resolving conflict.
○ Explain the various steps which are important in negotiation (see **RULES FOR NEGOTIATION**).
○ The worksheet **RULES FOR NEGOTIATION** could be given to the students, projected on the OHP, or displayed.
○ Comment on these rules and give an example of their use in resolving a conflict situation, e.g. a pupil never giving homework in on time.

● Phase II
○ Form pairs and decide who is to be A and B.

> A – You can't concentrate on your homework as your brother is playing his music loudly.
>
> B – You are A's brother and don't enjoy music unless it is played loudly.

○ Allow a few minutes for students to briefly role play the situation.
○ Give each student the worksheet **NEGOTIATION IN PRACTICE**.
○ Using their assumed roles, students complete section 1 of the worksheet.
○ This is done individually without reference to partners.
○ Students now:
  – Share with their partners what they have written.
  – Listen carefully to each other's suggestions.
  – Decide on a solution.
  – Complete section 2 of the form.
○ Repeat this procedure with the following situations:

> A – You are Mum and insist that B is home by 9 p.m.
> B – You are 14 years old and want to stay out after 9 p.m.

> A – You are late for class again today and receive a detention.
> B – You are the teacher, and are not prepared to accept A constantly arriving late for class.

Group Size: Pairs

Time: 30–40 minutes

Materials: The teacher requires:
○ worksheet **RULES FOR NEGOTIATION**

Each student requires:
○ worksheet **NEGOTIATION IN PRACTICE**

Notes:
Negotiation is a way of resolving conflicts so that everybody 'wins'. Essentially it is a process whereby the parties work to a solution which is acceptable to all. Negotiation can take place when all the parties involved:
– respect each other's situations
– see the conflict as a mutual problem to be solved
– are prepared to listen and compromise
– are not interested in 'winning at any cost'.

Students have already considered the importance of negotiation for successful conflict resolution and in this strategy they identify the skills required for this and apply them to conflict incidents.

The teacher may wish to comment on the 'I want . . . because . . .' section of the worksheet **NEGOTIATION IN PRACTICE**. The 'because . . .' looks at the person's motives and reasons for what he wants, e.g.
Mum: I want you home by 9 p.m. because I am concerned about your safety.
Son: I want to stay out later because my friends are allowed to.
Understanding each other's motives in this way increases the chances of Mum and her son resolving their conflict successfully.

● Phase III
○ Reconvene the class and discuss:
  – Did students find the negotiation strategy helpful? In what way?
  – Could this strategy be employed to resolve real-life conflicts?

Extension:
If it is appropriate, students could take issues that exist in the classroom and complete a negotiation exercise around them, e.g. homework deadlines, seating arrangements.

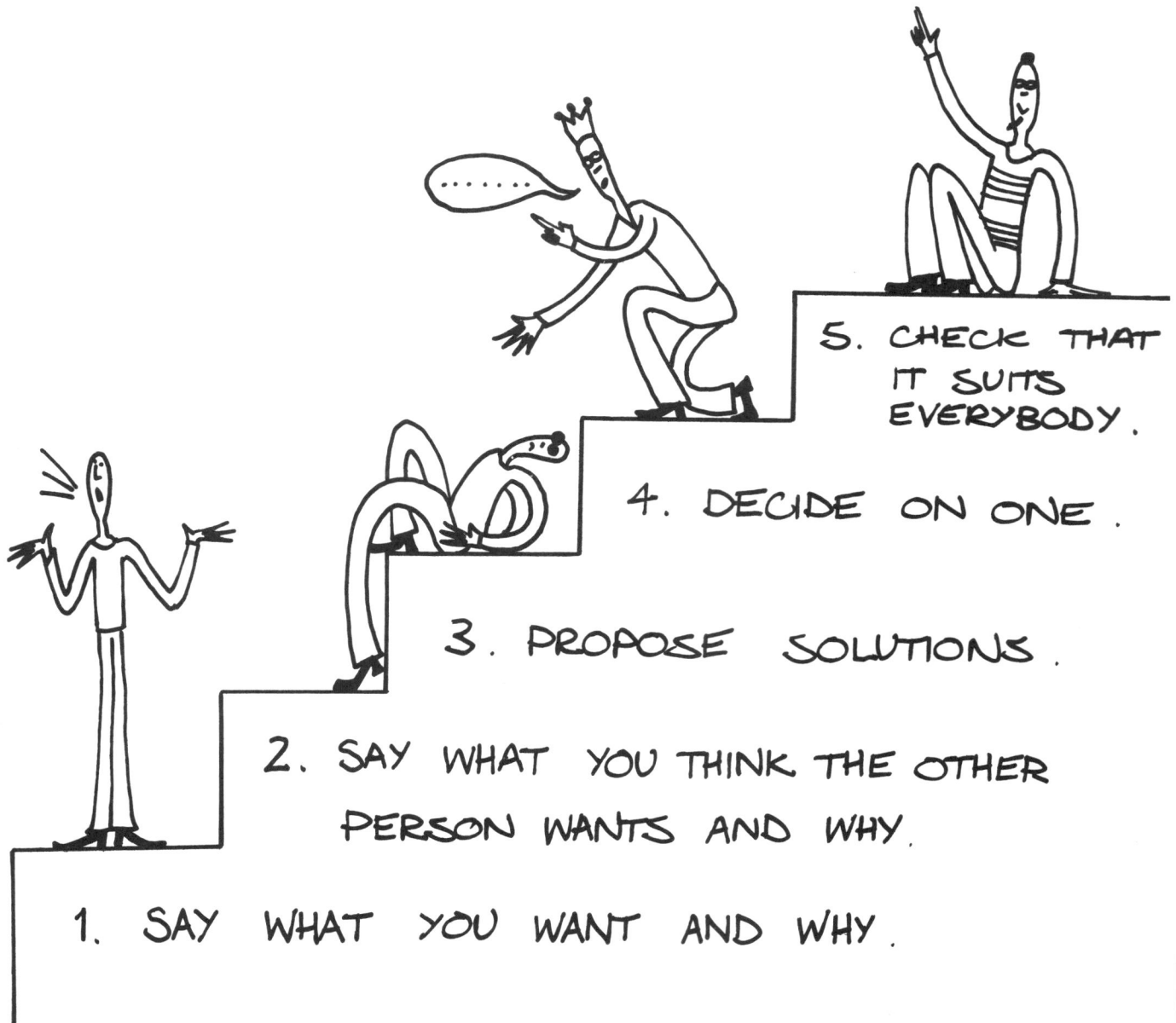

RULES FOR NEGOTIATION

5. CHECK THAT IT SUITS EVERYBODY.

4. DECIDE ON ONE.

3. PROPOSE SOLUTIONS.

2. SAY WHAT YOU THINK THE OTHER PERSON WANTS AND WHY.

1. SAY WHAT YOU WANT AND WHY.

Ⓟ © Shay McConnon 1990

NEGOTIATION IN PRACTICE

Name _____ Date _____

In your assumed role, complete section 1 of this sheet. It is important to give your reasons, e.g. *I want* peace and quiet *because* I have an exam on Monday.

Section 1

1 I want _____

because _____

2 I think you want _____

because _____

3 Here are my suggestions:

_____

_____

Now share what you have written with your partner. Listen to his/her suggestions, decide on a solution and then complete section 2 of this sheet.

Section 2

4 Let's decide to try _____

5 Does this suit everybody? YES/NO

NEGOTIATION IN PRACTICE

Name _____ Date _____

In your assumed role, complete section 1 of this sheet. It is important to give your reasons, e.g. *I want* peace and quiet *because* I have an exam on Monday.

Section 1

1 I want _____

because _____

2 I think you want _____

because _____

3 Here are my suggestions:

_____

_____

Now share what you have written with your partner. Listen to his/her suggestions, decide on a solution and then complete section 2 of this sheet.

Section 2

4 Let's decide to try _____

5 Does this suit everybody? YES/NO

Ⓟ © Shay McConnon 1990

Aim:
To provide students with the opportunity to practise the skills of negotiation and receive feedback on their use of these skills.

Procedure:

- **Phase I**
  - Form groups of 12.
  - 3 are to act as observers, 9 as players.
  - Each group appoints the 3 observers.
  - Each observer is assigned to 3 players and given an **OBSERVER'S SHEET**.
  - Give the remaining 9 students 1 **ROLE AND TASK CARD** each, plus 8 tokens each (2 of each colour).
  - Explain the task.
  - Each player attempts to achieve the objective outlined on her card by applying the negotiation skills learnt in the previous strategy.
  - The objectives involve acquiring, exchanging or giving away tokens.
  - Players are to barter and negotiate with each other in attempting to achieve their objectives.
  - Draw the observers' attention to the behaviours that are to be observed.
  - In their groups, players take it in turn to read out their **ROLE AND TASK CARD**.
  - At a signal, players begin negotiating.
  - Allow 8–12 minutes for this.

- **Phase II**
  - Observers now meet with the players they observed and offer feedback on their use of negotiation skills.
  - Reconvene the class and discuss:
    - Were any players successful in their negotiations? Why? Why not?
  - Invite the observers to comment on the good use of negotiation skills.

- **Phase III**
  - The original groups of 12 re-form and appoint 3 new observers.
  - Give each new observer an **OBSERVER'S SHEET**.
  - They give their **ROLE AND TASK CARDS** to the original observers.
  - Each group forms a circle, with the observers on the outside.
  - The tokens are handed in and four piles made – blue, red, yellow and green.
  - The banker invites the 6 players who want tokens to present a case, in turn, why the group should allocate tokens to their causes.
  - The group in the circle is to listen, discuss, negotiate and then decide which cause should be given priority.
  - That player is then given the required number of tokens.

Group Size: 12

Time:
Approximately 45 minutes

Materials:
Each player requires:
- 1 **ROLE AND TASK CARD**
- 2 blue tokens, 2 red tokens, 2 yellow tokens, 2 green tokens

Each observer requires:
- **OBSERVER'S SHEET**

- The group in the circle now decides on the next priority case, and so on.
- Allow 10–15 minutes for this.

- **Phase IV**
  - The observers now meet with the players they observed and offer feedback on their use of negotiation skills.
  - Reconvene the class and draw attention to:
    - good practice they observed
    - the moments when conflict was defused and how
    - behaviours and attitudes which helped the group to find a consensus.

Extensions:
1. Video record the negotiation exercise and during playback draw attention to the good use of negotiation skills.
2. In Phase I issue the players with various instructions, e.g. 'Be ruthless and demanding', 'Be prepared to compromise', and later discuss the consequences of such behaviours on the negotiation procedure.
3. Students could practise these negotiating skills by role playing conflict situations of concern to them.

Notes:

This strategy creates an opportunity for students to practise the skills of negotiation that have been identified in the previous strategy.

Tokens are needed for the negotiating exercise. These could be cut from blue, red, yellow and green card — 18 of each colour, 72 in all.

The size of the group can be changed by varying the number of observers or reducing the number of players. If there is a change in the number of players, the number of **ROLE AND TASK CARDS** and tokens will need to change accordingly.

In Phase I the point of the exercise is not that everyone should achieve their task but that each takes part in the negotiation process — to practise and be observed in the use of negotiation skills. It is deliberately designed so that players will probably not achieve their tasks; hence they will continue to negotiate and so practise the skills of negotiation.

Players should be discouraged from demanding tokens, being aggressive or argumentative. Players should give or exchange tokens only if they have been 'persuaded' that the other person has a greater need of them.

Comment on the **OBSERVER'S SHEET** and how it is to be completed. Explain to the players that the observers will be looking for evidence of the use of negotiating skills:
— saying what you want and why
— finding out what the other person wants
— suggesting solutions
— encouraging some form of agreement.
If necessary, as an example, the teacher could invite two students to carry out a negotiation in front of the class while he/she fills in an **OBSERVER'S SHEET**.

Phase III will allow most students to achieve their objectives. As it requires the group to reach a consensus decision, it is an ideal opportunity for students to demonstrate their use of negotiating skills.

ROLE AND TASK CARDS

You are a TV addict. Your set has broken and you are suffering palpitations and nervous twitches. You desperately need to buy a new TV.	**TV ADDICT** Cost of new TV:	B R Y G 5 2 2 3
Your father is dying. You urgently need to visit him.	**TRAVELLER** Cost of travel:	B Y R G 2 2 5 3
It is your birthday and you are celebrating by taking your boy/girlfriend out for a meal.	**BIRTHDAY** Cost of meal:	B R Y G 2 2 3 5
You want to raise money for the starving people of India. You want to send as much money as possible.	**INDIA FUND** 'Please give generously to me.'	
Your dog has been hit by a car and needs an operation.	**DOG OWNER** Vet's fees:	B R Y G 5 2 3 2
You have an incurable disease and only one month to live. You have always wanted to go for a ride in a helicopter.	**TERMINAL DISEASE** Cost of ride:	B R Y G 2 5 3 2
You are the banker. You are to colour-exchange tokens as requested by your clients, e.g. a red token for a blue token, etc.	**BANKER** 'I exchange tokens.'	
A TV appeal has raised a sum of money and your job is to distribute this to people in need (PIN).	**PIN AID** 'I give to people in need.'	
You are a millionaire. You listen carefully to people in need and are noted for your generosity to *genuine*, worthy causes.	**MILLIONAIRE** 'I give to worthy causes.'	

26

Ⓟ © Shay McConnon 1990

OBSERVER'S SHEET

Date _____ Observed by _____

Name _____

Name _____

Name _____

HELPFUL BEHAVIOURS

LISTENING

SAYING CLEARLY WHAT SHE/HE WANTS

FINDING OUT WHAT OTHERS WANT

SUGGESTING SOLUTIONS

UNHELPFUL BEHAVIOURS

AGGRESSIVE

DEMANDING

ARGUING

Each time you observe a particular behaviour, mark the appropriate box, e.g.   AGGRESSIVE |III|

OBSERVER'S SHEET

Date _____ Observed by _____

Name _____

Name _____

Name _____

HELPFUL BEHAVIOURS

LISTENING

SAYING CLEARLY WHAT SHE/HE WANTS

FINDING OUT WHAT OTHERS WANT

SUGGESTING SOLUTIONS

UNHELPFUL BEHAVIOURS

AGGRESSIVE

DEMANDING

ARGUING

Each time you observe a particular behaviour, mark the appropriate box, e.g.   AGGRESSIVE |III|

Ⓟ © Shay McConnon 1990

Aim: To help students identify a conflict in their lives which is causing concern and decide on ways of handling it.

Procedure:

- **Phase I**
  - Give each student the worksheet **CONFLICT IN MY LIFE**.
  - Explain how the worksheet is to be completed.
  - Allow time for students to complete it.
  - Form pairs.
  - Pairs take it in turn to share what they have written and in particular the three priority conflicts they have identified.
  - Students are free to pass.

- **Phase II**
  - Pairs decide who is to be A and B.
  - A decides on a priority conflict, i.e. 'A conflict I would like to do something about'.
  - Pairs now role play this conflict situation.
  - Allow 2–3 minutes for this.
  - Reverse roles and pairs play the situation again.
  - B decides on a priority conflict.
  - This is role-played then again roles are reversed.
  - Reconvene the class and discuss:
    - How did it feel to view the conflict from both perspectives?
    - Was it helpful?
    - Could this technique be used to resolve conflicts that exist in the students' lives? Any examples?

- **Phase III**
  - Give each student the worksheet **A PRIORITY CONFLICT**.
  - Explain how the worksheet is to be completed and if necessary read aloud an example of a completed worksheet.
  - Allow time for the worksheets to be completed.

- **Phase IV**
  - Students with similar conflict concerns form groups of 4–5.
  - Each takes it in turn to talk about his priority conflict and his analysis of the situation.
  - Students are to discuss with each other 'the steps I can take right now to improve the situation' and ask for suggestions and alternatives.
  - In the light of this discussion, students are to revise the 'steps I can take right now . . .'.

Group Size: Individuals; pairs; 4–5

Time: 50–60 minutes

Materials: Each student requires:
- worksheet **CONFLICT IN MY LIFE**
- worksheet **A PRIORITY CONFLICT**

Extensions:

1 Conclude the session by reconvening the class and inviting students to describe a conflict that is causing concern and share what they have decided to do about it with the class.
2 In small groups, students role play a conflict situation from their own lives. The group members give suggestions on ways to reduce this conflict. They then role play the situation again, incorporating these suggestions. In this way, the students prepare for and rehearse the actions they wish to adopt in the conflict situation.
3 Make available the **A SELF CONTRACT** and **SUCCESS!** worksheets (from Strategy 11) for students who wish to commit themselves in a more formal way to improving their conflict situation.
4 Students draw a graph to show conflict moments in their day, e.g.

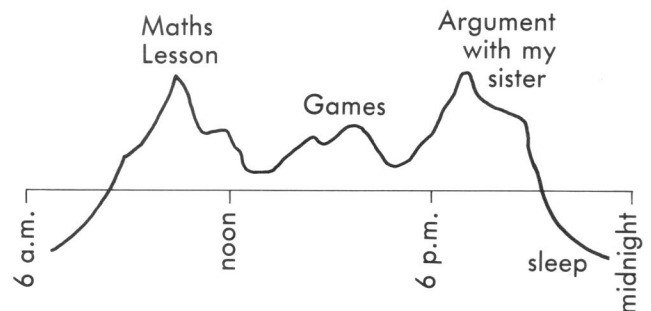

Notes:

The course progesses from the study of conflict and the practice of resolution skills to the application of these to the students' lives. Students are asked to identify conflicts which are causing concern, analyse them, become aware of the feelings generated and decide on ways for improving the situation.

The strategy works best if students have the opportunity to discuss their analysis, feelings and solutions for the conflict with those who have experienced similar conflicts. Hence the working groups of Phase IV should be composed of students who have similar conflict concerns. Encourage students to be practical and realistic in their suggestions for improving the conflict situation.

Time could be created at the beginning of the next few sessions to allow students to review progress and adopt new suggestions. The same procedure can be repeated for the other priority conflicts.

The worksheet **A PRIORITY CONFLICT** could be a useful tool for students who wish to resolve a conflict between themselves. Both parties need to agree on a procedure, e.g. each completes a worksheet; they exchange worksheets; each reads, without commenting, what the other has written; each takes it in turn to clarify what the other has written; they discuss with each other the steps that can be taken to improve the situation and, if appropriate, agree on a plan of action. (This procedure could be used to resolve conflicts within the class, both student/student and teacher/student conflicts. Some students might wish to use the worksheet **A PRIORITY CONFLICT** with parents, brothers/sisters, etc.)

CONFLICT IN MY LIFE

Name _____   Date _____

Note the source of the conflict and who you conflict with and then star the relevant box:
— 3 stars for conflict that causes a lot of upset
— 2 stars for conflict that causes some upset
— 1 star for conflict that causes little upset
(Use the blanks in the grid for items/people of your choice.)

	Mum	Dad	Brother	Sister	Boy/Girlfriend	Grandparents	Friends	Teachers	Neighbours	
TIDINESS										
TV										
HAIRSTYLE										
BEING LATE										
BEDROOM										
ATTITUDES										
LANGUAGE										
CLOTHES										
MY FUTURE										
FRIENDS										
BEHAVIOUR										
HUMOUR										
SCHOOL										
HOMEWORK										
MONEY										
POLITICS										
RELIGION										
HOUSEWORK										

HAIRSTYLE?

?!!*"

LANGUAGE?

MONSTER RAVING LOONY MAD PARTY

POLITICS?

Three conflicts I would like to do something about are:

1 _____

2 _____

3 _____

30

Ⓟ © Shay McConnon 1990

A PRIORITY CONFLICT

Name _____

A conflict I would like to do something about is:

_____

_____

Who is involved in the conflict?

_____

Because of the conflict I feel
(circle your feelings):

disappointed   upset

rejected   sad

frustrated   frightened

surprised   ashamed

confused   depressed

worried   angry

Because of the conflict the other person probably feels:

disappointed   upset

rejected   sad

frustrated   frightened

surprised   ashamed

confused   depressed

worried   angry

I want _____

_____

because _____

_____

The other person wants _____

_____

because _____

_____

What I can do about the conflict is:

★ _____

_____

★ _____

_____

★ _____

_____

What the other person might do about the conflict is:

★ _____

_____

★ _____

_____

★ _____

_____

The steps I can take right now to improve the conflict situation are:

1 _____

2 _____

3 _____

31

Ⓟ © Shay McConnon 1990

Aim: To draw students' attention to conflicts that can be avoided and to ways of preventing them.

Procedure:

- **Phase I**
  - Form groups of 3–4.
  - Give each group the worksheet **MIKE'S DAY (1)** and **(2)**.
  - Each group chooses a secretary and a spokesperson.
  - Each group studies the picture-strip of Mike's day on worksheet **(1)**, decides with whom he is in conflict and why, and suggests how he could avoid these conflicts.
  - The secretary writes the group's answers on worksheet **(2)**.
  - Reconvene the class and invite each spokesperson to report back.

- **Phase II**
  - Give each student the worksheet **REDUCING CONFLICT**.
  - Explain the worksheet and allow time for students to complete it.
  - Re-form to the original groups of 3–4.
  - Students take it in turn to share what they have written.
  - Students are free to pass.

- **Phase III**
  - Reconvene the class and discuss:
    - What are the consequences of conflict in Mike's life?
    - Is Mike a happy person?
    - Are the conflicts really avoidable in his life?
    - Are all conflicts avoidable?
    - Do many 'avoidable' conflicts exist in this classroom? What are they?
    - What can be done about them?

Extensions:

1 Invite students to role play the various episodes in Mike's day. These students could also be asked to decide how Mike could have behaved to avoid the conflicts and then role play these.
2 Students rewrite/redraw Mike's day, replacing the conflict situations with positive moments.
3 Provide students with a list of conflict situations which they are to categorise into 'avoidable' and 'unavoidable' conflicts.

Group Size: 3–4

Time: 30–40 minutes

Materials: Each group requires:
- worksheet **MIKE'S DAY (1)**
- worksheet **MIKE'S DAY (2)**

Each student requires:
- worksheet **REDUCING CONFLICT**

Notes:

This strategy looks at ways students can minimise conflict in their lives. Although conflict may be an inevitable part of life, some conflicts can be prevented. This strategy draws students' attention to 'avoidable conflicts', and asks them to identify such conflicts in their lives and consider ways of preventing them.

The opportunity could be taken to focus on 'avoidable conflicts' that exist in the classroom, both student/student conflicts and teacher/student conflicts.

MIKE'S DAY (1)

1 Home: 8.10 a.m.

2 School: 10.00 a.m.

3 School: 12.45 p.m.

4 Home: 5.00 p.m.

5 Home: 6.30 p.m.

6 Youth club: 9.00 p.m.

7 Home: 11.30 p.m.

Ⓟ © Shay McConnon 1990

MIKE'S DAY (2)

1 Mike is in conflict with _____

   because _____

   He could avoid the conflict if he _____

   _____

2 Mike is in conflict with _____

   because _____

   He could avoid the conflict if he _____

   _____

3 Mike is in conflict with _____

   because _____

   He could avoid the conflict if he _____

   _____

4 Mike is in conflict with _____

   because _____

   He could avoid the conflict if he _____

   _____

5 Mike is in conflict with _____

   because _____

   He could avoid the conflict if he _____

   _____

6 Mike is in conflict with _____

   because _____

   He could avoid the conflict if he _____

   _____

7 Mike is in conflict with _____

   because _____

   He could avoid the conflict if he _____

   _____

Ⓟ © Shay McConnon 1990

REDUCING CONFLICT

Name _____   Date _____

The conflicts I share with Mike:

_____

_____

_____

_____

_____

I can avoid these by:

_____

_____

_____

_____

_____

Other 'avoidable conflicts' in my life are:

_____

_____

_____

_____

_____

I can avoid these by:

_____

_____

_____

_____

_____

If there was less conflict in my life I _____

_____

I shall reduce conflict in my life if I _____

_____

If there was less conflict in the world _____

_____

35

Ⓟ © Shay McConnon 1990

Aim: To help students identify target behaviours and commit themselves to these using a structured plan for behaviour change.

Procedure:

- **Phase I**
  - Form groups of 4–5.
  - Give each student the worksheet **ME**.
  - Each group decides on a focal person.
  - The focal person asks each group member to assess his conflict management style.
  - Group members begin with 'withdrawal' as a management style and say which box on the assessment sheet they would tick for the focal person, i.e. very often, fairly often etc.
  - After listening to what the group members have said, the focal person ticks a box on the assessment sheet which he feels reflects him.
  - Students take it in turn to be the focal person and work through the list of management styles and the skills of negotiation.
  - Students now complete the remaining sections of the worksheet.

- **Phase II**
  - Each student decides on a priority goal he wishes to work towards.
  - Explain the elements of successful goal achievement (see Notes).
  - Give each student the worksheets **A SELF CONTRACT** and **SUCCESS!**
  - Comment on the worksheets and how and when they are to be completed.
  - Students may work on their own, with a partner of their choice or in small groups.
  - Allow time for the students to fill in the worksheet **A SELF CONTRACT**.
  - Students may ask for ideas and support from other group members in achieving this goal.
  - Set a future date for students to review and share progress.
  - When students have achieved their goal they complete the worksheet **SUCCESS!**

Extensions:
1 In groups of 4–6, students take it in turn to offer a goal for the group's consideration. The group brainstorms for ideas on how to achieve this goal and the student uses these ideas to complete the **A SELF CONTRACT** worksheet.
2 Students write a goal on a slip of paper. These are folded and handed to the teacher who mixes them and selects one at random. The class brainstorms for ideas on how to achieve this goal. In this way students can get ideas and help without revealing their identities.

Group Size: 4–5; varies

Time: 40–50 minutes

Materials: Each student requires:
- worksheet **ME**
- worksheet **A SELF CONTRACT**
- worksheet **SUCCESS!**

3 In small groups each student writes his goal on a sheet of paper. This is passed to the person on the right who writes suggestions for achieving this goal on the bottom of the sheet. This is folded over and passed to the next person on the right. This continues until each student has his original sheet again. The student now uses these ideas in deciding on a plan for goal achievement.
4 Create time at the beginning of the next few sessions for students to review their goals and the plans for achieving them.

Notes:

This strategy provides students with the opportunity to decide on a conflict resolution skill they would like to improve on and draw up a plan of action for achieving it.

This is not a negative exercise but a moment to highlight those skills students are good at, as well as drawing attention to those requiring attention.

The following five stages provide a structure for successful goal achievement:

(a) *Goal:* Warn against the goal being set too high. It is to be realistic and attainable. The goal: 'I am going to reduce conflict in my life' is too vague to be of much value. 'I am going to lessen the conflict I have with Mr Smith' has more meaning as a goal.

(b) *Plan:* The steps to achieving the goal are to be practical and workable, e.g. 'I shall (i) hand my homework in on time, (ii) do my homework the evening it is set and (iii) get someone to help me when I don't understand the work.'

(c) *Support system:* Who is going to help the student achieve this goal? What part can peers, home, staff play? These people should be consulted if they are to support the student. 'Zia is going to help me with my homework.'

(d) *Time:* A realistic time should be set, which will vary considerably from person to person, e.g. 'I shall start immediately and hope that Mr Smith and I will be getting on better by the end of the month.'

(e) *Celebration:* The student rewards himself when the goal has been achieved, e.g. 'I will hire a video and invite John and Shahnaz around to watch it', and fills in the **SUCCESS!** worksheet.

Some long-term goals may require several short-term goals to be realised first, so make the **A SELF CONTRACT** and **SUCCESS!** worksheets available to students as and when necessary.

Goal setting should not be seen as a one-off moment but as a continuous process with students monitoring their own and each other's progress, reviewing goals, plans and support systems.

This structured plan for behaviour change together with the **A SELF CONTRACT** and **SUCCESS!** worksheets can be used at other times during this course when students decide on target behaviours.

ME

Name _____   Date _____

My Conflict Management Style

	VERY OFTEN	FAIRLY OFTEN	SOMETIMES	NOT OFTEN	ALMOST NEVER
WITHDRAWAL (I run away)					
AGGRESSION (I bully to get what I want)					
MEDIATION (I ask another to help)					
NEGOTIATION ('Let's solve this together')					

My conflict management style generally is: _____

My Rating as a Negotiator

Do I:

	VERY OFTEN	FAIRLY OFTEN	SOMETIMES	NOT OFTEN	ALMOST NEVER
LISTEN?					
SAY CLEARLY WHAT I WANT?					
FIND OUT WHAT THE OTHER PERSON WANTS?					
SUGGEST SOLUTIONS?					
COMPROMISE WHEN APPROPRIATE?					
CHECK OUT WITH OTHERS?					

I am a good negotiator because:

1 _____

2 _____

I would be a better negotiator if:

1 _____

2 _____

My priority goals are:

★ _____

★ _____

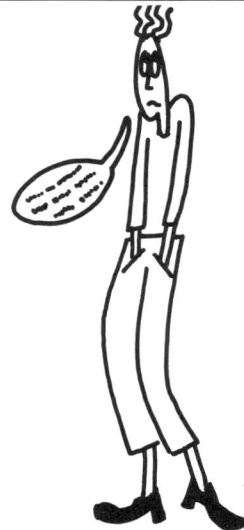

DO I SAY CLEARLY WHAT I WANT?

Ⓟ © Shay McConnon 1990

A SELF CONTRACT

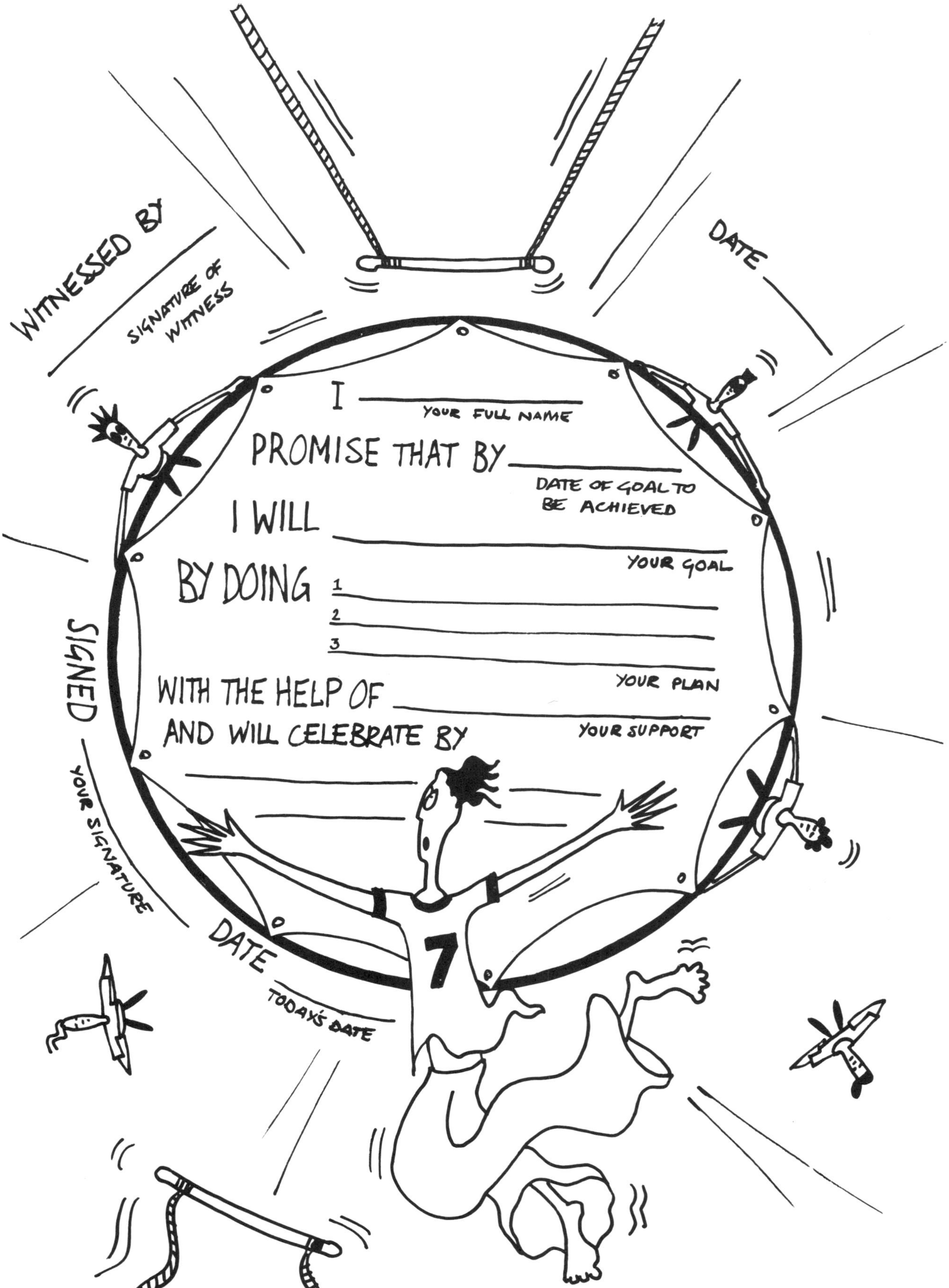

I _____ YOUR FULL NAME

PROMISE THAT BY _____
DATE OF GOAL TO BE ACHIEVED

I WILL _____ YOUR GOAL

BY DOING
1 _____
2 _____
3 _____ YOUR PLAN

WITH THE HELP OF _____ YOUR SUPPORT
AND WILL CELEBRATE BY
_____
_____

WITNESSED BY
SIGNATURE OF WITNESS

DATE

SIGNED
YOUR SIGNATURE

DATE
TODAY'S DATE

Ⓟ © Shay McConnon 1990

Name _____

SUCCESS!

MY GOAL _____

_____

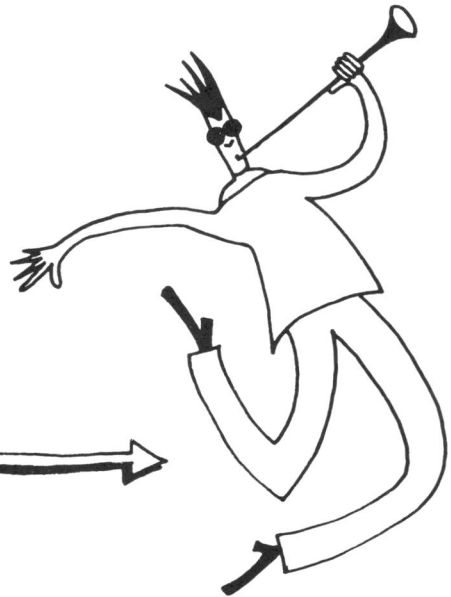

MY PLAN
OF ACTION
1 _____
2 _____
3 _____

SUPPORTED BY _____

WATER

DATE ACHIEVED _____

CELEBRATED BY _____
_____

Ⓟ © Shay McConnon 1990

12 HOW HAVE WE GOT ON? ■■■■

Aim: To review the course on **CONFLICT** and to assess the student's response to it.

Procedure:

• Phase I
○ Divide the class into two circles, an inner and an outer circle, with the students facing each other in pairs.
○ Tell the students to discuss: 'What I liked about this course' with their partners.
○ Allow 2–3 minutes for this.
○ Inner circle moves to the left and students now discuss: 'What I disliked about this course'.
○ Continue this procedure with the following discussion topics:
   – Why I enjoyed/didn't enjoy this course.
   – Suggestions I have for improving the course.
   – The most important thing I have learnt probably is . . .
   – I can reduce conflict in my life by . . .
   – I am good at negotiating because . . .

• Phase II
○ Give each student the worksheet **HOW HAVE I GOT ON?**
○ Comment as necessary.
○ Students are to complete these working individually.
○ The completed sheets are collected and handed to the teacher.

Extensions:
1 Turn the phrases on the worksheet into questions, e.g. 'Did you enjoy the course – a lot? a bit? not at all?' etc. and write each question on a large sheet of paper. Display these around the room. Students are to wander around the room answering the questions by writing on the sheets of paper. Conclude by commenting on each sheet and inviting further comments.
2 Students complete and share a list of incomplete sentences which will help them review the course, e.g. 'I liked this course because . . .', 'I am pleased I did . . .', 'I would like to do more of . . .', 'I learned . . .'.

Group Size: Varies

Time: 30–40 minutes

Materials: Each student requires:
○ worksheet **HOW HAVE I GOT ON?**

Notes:
Evaluation is an essential function in any education programme. It enables teachers to monitor progress and provides them with feedback on the effectiveness of the programme, course materials and strategies. Ideally evaluation should be regarded as a continuous process and not an isolated procedure tackled at the end of a course.

Young people are inclined to find evaluation difficult and a written questionnaire often gets limited results. So Phase I begins with an activity intended to stimulate students' memories, feelings and judgement. This is then followed by the questionnaire.

HOW HAVE I GOT ON ?

Name _____   Date _____

I have found this course useful:

very └─┴─┴─┴─┴─┘ not at all

I have enjoyed this course:

a lot └─┴─┴─┴─┴─┘ not at all

CIRCLE THE WORDS YOU FEEL APPLY TO THE COURSE:

confusing   stressful   stimulating   depressing   entertaining   disappointing

irrelevant   fun   relevant   difficult   helpful   relaxing

easy   interesting

Two things I disliked about the course:

1 ....

2 ....

Two things I liked about the course:

1 ....

2 ....

Rate the following:

worksheets   very useful └─┴─┴─┴─┴─┘ not at all

discussion   └─┴─┴─┴─┴─┘

teacher talking   └─┴─┴─┴─┴─┘

video (if used)   └─┴─┴─┴─┴─┘

role-play   └─┴─┴─┴─┴─┘

Probably the most important thing
I have learnt is:

....

....

My suggestions for improving the course are:

....

....

I CAN REDUCE CONFLICT IN MY LIFE BY:

....

....

....

....

The goals I have set myself are:

....

....

....

I am good at negotiating because:

....

....

42

Ⓟ © Shay McConnon 1990

APPENDIX: STRATEGIES FOR HANDLING PERSISTENT CONFLICT

Here are two strategies that can be used in situations where there is persistent conflict between students. They can help students to listen to, and focus on, each other's perspectives. They allow students to express their anger and resentment in a way which is 'safe' and acceptable, and to look for positive ways of resolving the conflict.

The success of these strategies requires the willingness of both parties to try it, a sensitive and firm mediator and a quiet place. They should not be carried out in front of other students as part of a class exercise.

Although useful and positive strategies, they should be used with caution and only when both parties consent.

Strategy 1: Paraphrasing

The students in disagreement are to sit with a mediator. The mediator explains the procedure: Before anyone is allowed to speak, she or he is to restate what the previous speaker has said to that person's satisfaction.

The students in conflict are now invited to talk to each other about the source of the conflict and their associated feelings. The mediator is to ensure that the procedure is adhered to.

If there is some agreement on how each would like their relationship to be improved, the mediator focuses on ways to make this happen which are acceptable to both parties. If appropriate, the mediator draws up a contract for both parties to sign.

Strategy 2: Share it!

A mediator gives each party the worksheet **SHARE IT!**, which they complete and exchange. Each now reads what the other has written. No comments are allowed at this stage.

Each takes it in turn to clarify and check out what the other has written. If there is some agreement on how each would like their relationship to be improved, the mediator focuses on ways to make this happen which are acceptable to both parties. If appropriate, the mediator draws up a contract for both parties to sign.

SHARE IT!

BE HONEST.
DON'T TAKE TOO LONG.
WRITE EVERYTHING YOU FEEL.
WRITE ALL THE THINGS THAT COME TO MIND.
GET ALL YOUR ANGER/RESENTMENT ON TO THIS SHEET.
YOU ARE FREE TO DESTROY THIS SHEET LATER.

ME	YOU
You annoy me when . . .	I probably annoy you when I . . .
Then I feel . . .	Then you probably feel . . .
What I would like to happen is . . .	What you would probably like to happen is . . .
I can help by . . .	You can help by . . .

44

Ⓟ © Shay McConnon 1990